# Contents:

# Playing With The Dog

Joanna Bernat

# Soldiers March

Joanna Bernat

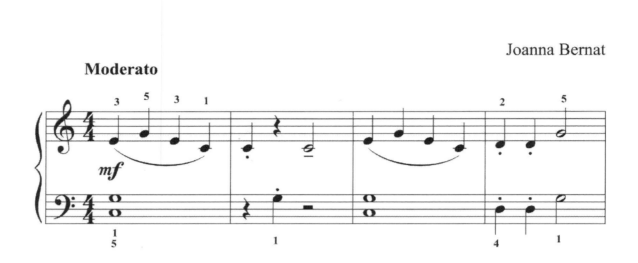

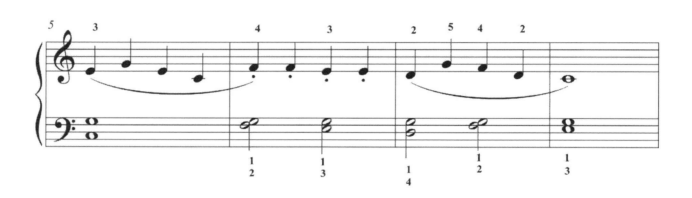

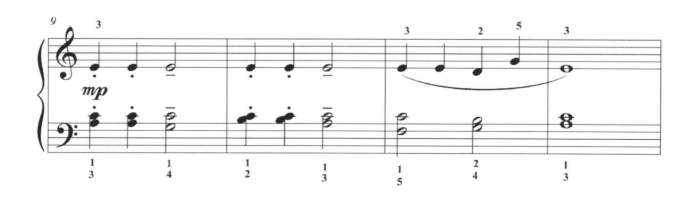

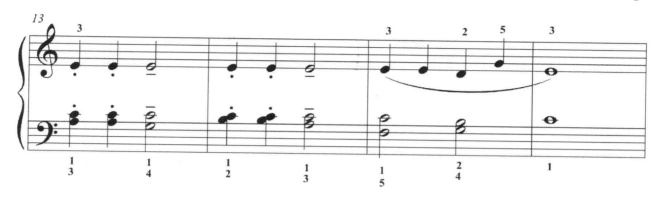

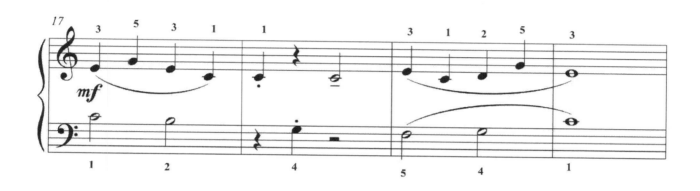

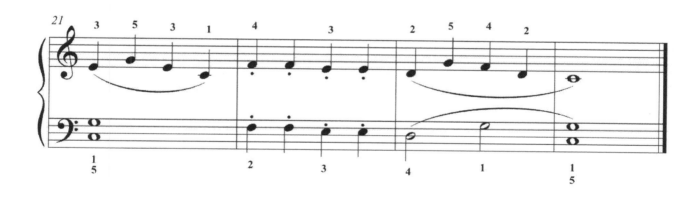

4

# Night Forest

Joanna Bernat

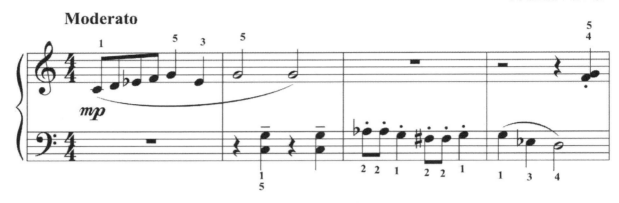

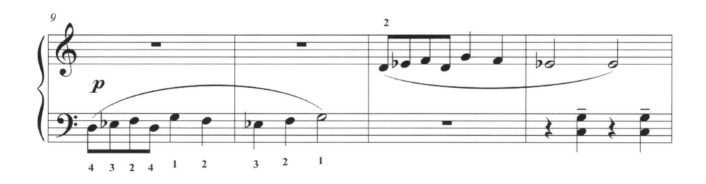

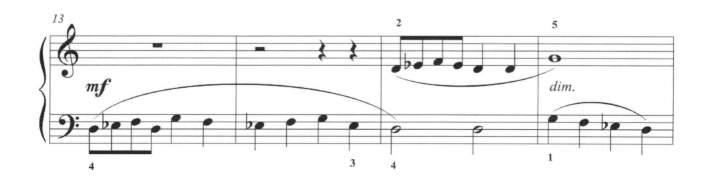

# Cars On The Road

Joanna Bernat

# Skipping Rope

**Andante**

Joanna Bernat

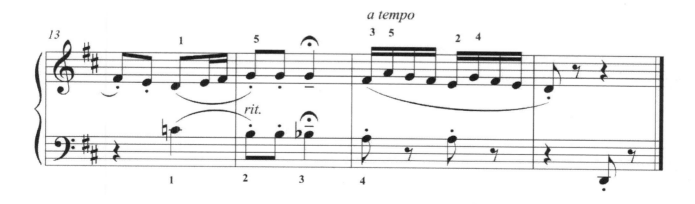

# In The Old Days

**Moderato**

Joanna Bernat

# Jugglers

Joanna Bernat

# A Thief

Joanna Bernat

**Allegro**

# A Guest From Space

Joanna Bernat

**Moderato**

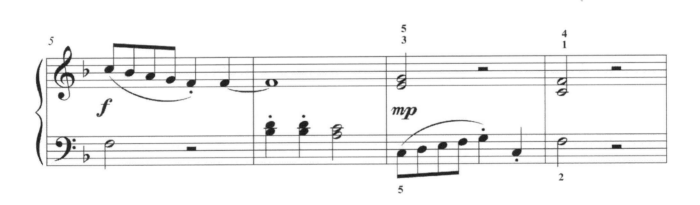

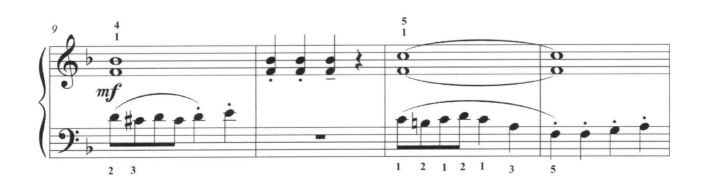

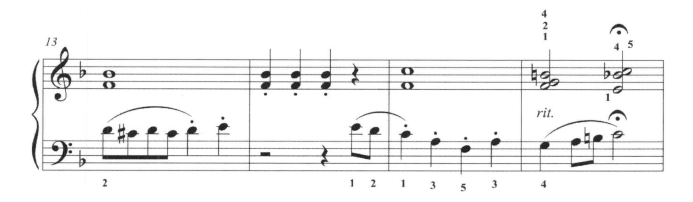

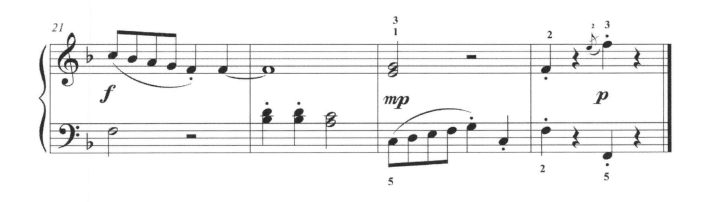

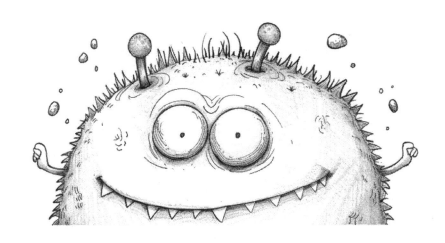

# A Sad Puppet

Joanna Bernat

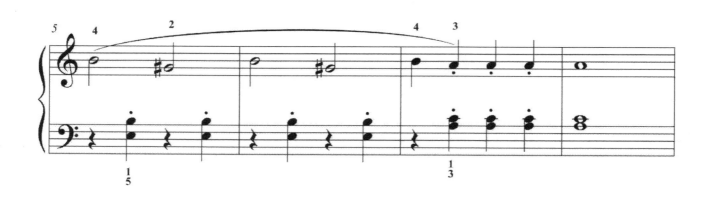

# March Of The Ducklings

Joanna Bernat

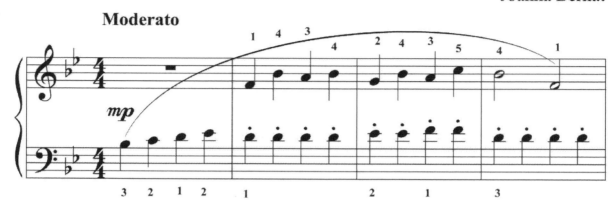

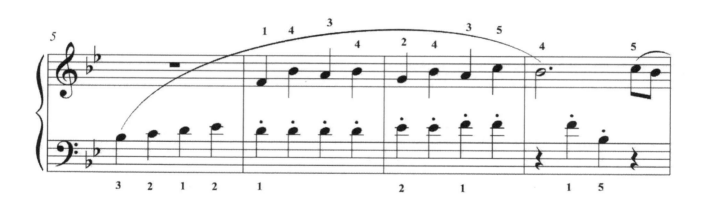

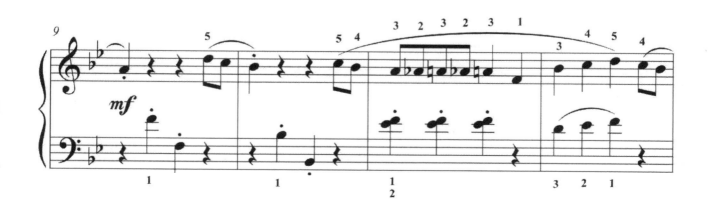

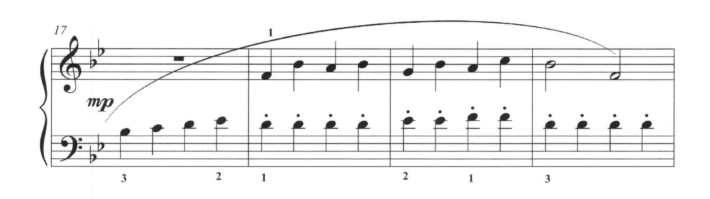

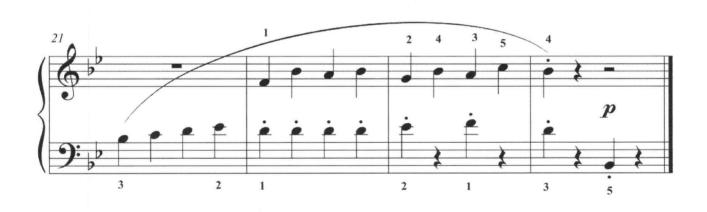

# The Grand Marche

Joanna Bernat

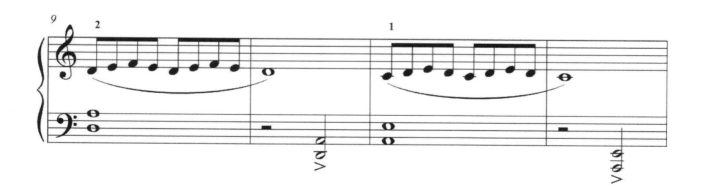

# A Trip To The Moon

Joanna Bernat

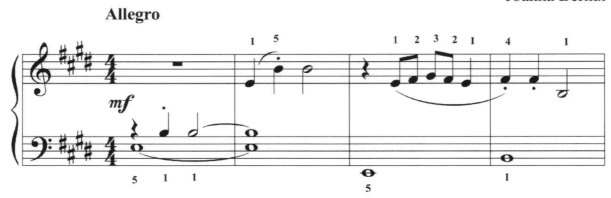

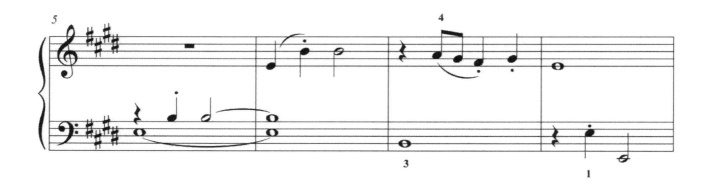

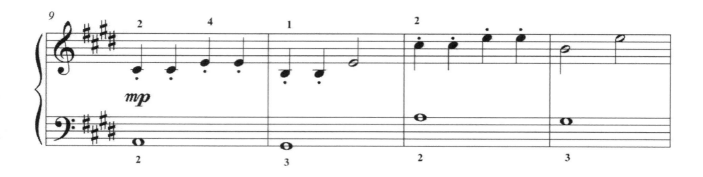

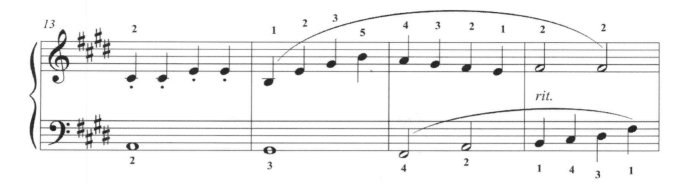

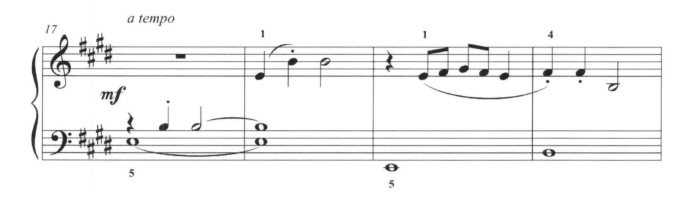

# Scottish Dance

Joanna Bernat

**Vivace**

# Cats' Mischiefs

Joanna Bernat

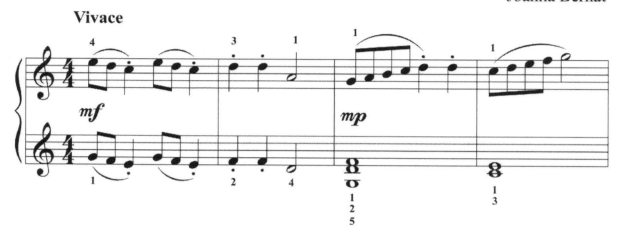

Printed in Great Britain
by Amazon

44961544R00015